In Praise of Cats

An Anthology

Compiled by Dorothy Foster
Illustrated by Alan Daniel

BEAUFORT BOOKS
New York • Toronto

©1974 Musson Book Company
©Illustrations Alan Daniel 1974

Library of Congress Cataloging in Publication Data
Main entry under title:

In praise of cats.

1. Cats–Poetry.   I. Foster, Dorothy.
PN6110.C315   1983   808.81'936   82-19733
ISBN 0-8253-0127-0

Published in the United States by Beaufort Books.
New York. Published simultaneously in Canada by
Musson

Printed in Canada

To Epimetheus:
The Cat
who
inspired
the work.

In Praise of Cats

CONTENTS

INTRODUCTION

The poet's purpose in most poems about cats is to praise him for various reasons: for his beauty, his agility, his insouciance, and, especially, for his value as a companion. This also is the purpose of this anthology: to praise the cat and to call attention to his attributes. The purpose of the anthology also parallels the classical purpose of poetry: to delight and to teach. It is believed this collection will be a source of joy and delight to those who number among the ranks of cat lovers. It is hoped this collection will help instruct those who have not opened their hearts to the feline, or who consider him at best a poor substitute for the dog.

In one of the poems included in this collection, *Singular Injustice*, Janet Lloyd muses on the peculiarity of those who "mock the spinster with her cat, / But beam through sentimental fog/Each time the bachelor walks his dog." This attitude had its origin centuries ago, when cats were associated with evil and witchcraft, and any cat owner was suspect. Attitudes are slow to change, even when the reasons for them have been erased from memory by time. However, cats have not always been an object of superstition and distrust. In ancient Egypt the role of the cat in society was at its zenith. The animal was held to be sacred, and was revered as a goddess. Cats were believed to be related to fertility, possibly because of their startling prolificacy, and were thought to exert power over weather and crops, much like the Greek goddess Demeter, or her Roman counterpart, Ceres. Their supposed powers in this regard may have sprung partially from their ability to keep fields and grain sheds free of rodents. When an Egyptian cat died, reverence for him demanded embalming and stately entombment. It is a pity that no poems from this era can be found. A paean to a cat-goddess must represent the height of poetic praise to the animal.

From Egypt the cat was transported to Rome, and the Romans brought the domesticated cat to Britain, although Britain did have a small wild cat of its own at the time. The usefulness of cats is apparent in many of the poems in this collection. The duty of the sixth-century cat in *The Cat and the Partridge* was to catch mice. Pangur, the eighth-century cat, was a "master of the death of mice," but his function as the scholar's companion and comrade in daily pursuits was his chief value. A highly unusual aspect of this poem is the warm friendship shown for a cat at a time when cats were associated with witches. Perhaps the poet's isolation as a scholar also isolated him from the suspicious eyes of the public. Cats were thought to be in league with the devil, or evil spirits, along with witches, their human counterparts. Witches sometimes worked their magic while in cat form, and cats executed diabolical deeds for their evil owners. The old wives' tale professing that a cat will suck a baby's breath has its origin in the belief that cats were suckled by the witches who owned them, as well as in the belief that a cat, or a witch in cat-disguise, may be impelled by evil spirits to destroy infants. This fear of cats in relation to babies and small children persists in the twentieth century, although the reason for the fear has been obscured.

Understandably then, no poems about cats written in Europe were found from the time of the anonymous poem in praise of Pangur to Joachim du Bellay's *Epitaph on a Pet Cat* written in sixteenth-century France. It is known, however, that in Wales in the eleventh century the value of the cat was recognized by law, and cat prices were set, such as one penny for a kitten, two pennies for a kitten with open eyes, and four pennies for a cat known to have caught one mouse. The Prince of Wales kept cats to catch mice in his granaries, and to kill one of them meant a severe fine for the transgressor.

Written references to cats during this period are rare. About 1393 Chaucer refers unflatteringly to the cat in *The Wife of Bath's Prologue:*

> Thou seydest this, that I was lyk a cat;
> For whoso wolde senge a cattes skyn,
> Thanne wolde the cat wel dwellen in his inn;
> And if the cattes skyn be slyk and gay,
> She wol nat dwelle in house half a day,
> But forth she wole, er any day be dawed
> To shewe hir skyn, and goon a-caterwawed.
> This is to seye, if I be gay, sir shrewe,
> I wol renne out, my borel for to shewe.

The Wife resents the comparison to the vain, carousing creature.

In 1387, John de Trevisa translated from an Old English source:

> The catte is a beast of uncertain heare [hair] and colour, for somme catte is white, some rede, some blacke, some skewed [piebald] and speckled in the fete and in the face and in the eares. He is a beste in youth, swyfte, plyaunte, and mery, and lepeth and reseth [rusheth] on all thynge that is to fore him; and is led by a strawe and playeth therwith. He is a right hevy beast in aege, and ful slepy, and lyeth slily in wait for myce. And he maketh a ruthefull noyse and gastfull, wahn one proffreth to fyghte with another, and he falleth on his owne fete whan he falleth out of high places.

While cats were not normally kept as household pets during the Middle Ages, their usefulness was acknowledged, and de Trevisa gives us a detailed outline of their behaviour and habits. But the status of the cat has at this time inverted. He is no longer a sign of fertility and growth, but a sign of sterility and evil. Witches were thought to use cats to inflict the curse of barrenness, surely a complete reversal from the Egyptian belief in their powers of fertility and growth.

Elegies on the death of cats prevail in cat poem history. Edgar Allan Poe said melancholy is the most legitimate of tones for poetry, death is the most melancholy topic, and since beauty is the province of the poem, he believed: "the death, then, of a beautiful woman is, unquestionably, the most poetical topic in the world—and equally is it beyond doubt that the lips best suited for such topic are those of a bereaved lover." Lips of bereaved poets have eulogized the death of their beloved pets, the loss of their beautiful friendships, for centuries, in tones almost as touching and melancholy as any lament by lover for his beloved. The earliest found is the ninth-century Arabic translation, written by Ibn Alalaf Alnaharwany. The early sixteenth-century elegy on Belaud written by du Bellay must mark the bare beginnings of the acceptance of the cat as a friend and object of beauty. It is a sign that the superstitions of the Dark Ages are gradually fading away in the growing light of the Renaissance.

Although the cat was usually not kept as a household pet through the seventeenth century, succeeding poems do not reflect this fact, but perhaps the more expansive spirit of the poet allowed him to reject superstitions connected with cats before his less enlightened neighbors. Presidents apparently do not share the special spirit of the poet, since Abraham Lincoln, the 16th president of the United States, from 1861 to 1865, was the first president to have a cat as a pet at the White House, while poets dating from the sixteenth century enjoyed the cat's company. Christopher Smart, Thomas Gray, William Cowper, John Keats, William Wordsworth, Matthew Arnold, Christina Rossetti, Paul Verlaine, and Thomas Hardy are among the more illustrious of poets collected here who enjoyed and loved cats through the nineteenth-century period. Edgar Allan Poe also owned a cat, of the large tortoiseshell variety, who slept on his ailing wife's chest to keep warm when Poe could ill afford the price of fuel.

The first cat show was held in London in the Crystal Palace in 1871, under the direction of Mr. Harrison Weir, and in this exhibition are grounded the roots of the cat fancy enthusiasm of today. Common elements of the enthusiasm in the twentieth century are pet shops, elaborately run shows, toys and clothing for cats, veterinarians, vaccinations, operations, health insurance, and special burial grounds for cats and other pets. And the cat has captured the attention, and probably the hearts, of serious artists of the twentieth century, including D.H. Lawrence, H.P. Lovecraft, William Butler Yeats, William Carlos Williams and Louis MacNeice.

Twentieth century poets prove the cat lends himself as an easy and versatile subject for a variety of types of poetry. The use of an animal with human characteristics is a well-known comic device. Don Marquis gets uproarious results where mehitabel's common-cat habits are indistinguishable from the habits of the people she used to be. The cat lends himself better to this device than other animals because of his near-human characteristics, such as moodiness, fastidiousness, and independence, and characteristics that humans envy, such as the insouciance and zest for life of mehitabel.

The delicacy and grace of the cat makes him a perfect subject for the light, well-balanced verse of poets such as A. S. F. Tessimond and Martha Ostenso. The swift, light touch of the latter reminds one of the delicate haiku collected here from the seventeenth and eighteenth centuries.

A change in elegies on cats occurred after the nineteenth century. Earlier elegies were gentle, and concentrated on the virtues of the dead cat and the cat as part of nature. The pastoral tradition is not present in the elegies of the twentieth century, such as those of H. P. Lovecraft and Louis MacNeice, which instead reflect a dread of progress and its ramifications. "Damn'd be this harsh mechanick age/That whirls us fast and faster" writes Lovecraft as he mourns the death of Oscar; and this lament is echoed by MacNeice as he experiences a horrible vision of his now dead pet struggling for survival and the path to home through "all the wheels/Of all the jeeps, trucks, trams, motor-bicycles, buses, sports cars." Morals were present in earlier cat poem history, from Alnaharwany's: "And curst the dainty where we find/ Destruction lurking in the dish," to Cowper's: "Beware of too sublime a sense/Of your own worth and consequence!". But these were morals of a more individual nature than the more universal condemnations of the twentieth century. Cats in any century are natural subjects for poems that draw a moral conclusion, because the wanderlust of some and the curiosity of many make them easy victims in situations where sagacity in forethought is required.

The attitude toward the cat in the twentieth century, along with his status in society, is mixed, as the attitude toward him historically is mixed. While his status in society has fluctuated over the centuries, it is interesting to note that his status in poetry has not. The poet has steadfastly considered the cat a worthy comrade. We have considered poetry about cats from the past, and poetry about cats from the present, and have considered the changing attitude toward them at the same time. Keeping in mind other common elements of life in the 1970s, it would be interesting and humorous to delve into an imaginary future, to see what ensuing years hold for cats, and for cat poetry. In an era of freedom movements such as the Women's Liberation Movement, which encourages women to leave their homes and find self-expression elsewhere, and the Canine Liberation League and Front, which beseeches us to unharness our dogs and let them roam at will, one wonders what, if any, developments will arise in the cat world. A look at the past and the character of the cat provides a quick glimpse of the future, where it is easy to see that the cat population is one constituency that will never be moved to mob action and the depersonalization that accompanies life in the crowd. The cat is not a joiner. And what other freedoms does he need? Each cat will continue to uphold a personal vision of himself as staunch individualist, monarch of all he surveys, free at all times to act as he pleases. One welcome addition for cats of the future would be facilities for those who are lost, strayed, or travelling, such as the missions, soup kitchens, and hostels available now for lost, strayed, or travelling humans. A cat on the move would be able then to obtain a free meal or a warm spot to sleep, if he chooses.

Poets have always recognized the free spirit of the cat, and while the general attitude toward cats may easily change in the distant future, it is safe to assume that the status of cats in poetry will remain unchanged. The poet's steady vision of the cat as individual, friend, and object of beauty will not waver.

DOROTHY FOSTER

The Proud
Mysterious Cat

A Cat

How many ages
Of Chinese ancestry
In the fine pages
Of your sleek history
Must there be, feline,
Tortuous mystery?
Skeins of the night that
Silkened the sky
Over dusky pagodas
Glimmering lie
Down your long sides;
And, thinner than water,
Like water glides
Your bland shadow
Along the floor.
How many cinnamon
Blossoms bore
Delicate shade through
Nightingaled hours,
In that remoter
Life that was yours
Down by the yellow,
Asian sea,
In lustrous, mellow
Antiquity?
In towers of jade
And minarets ashen
With dawn, did an idol
Dream and fashion
Your lithe and beautiful
Demoniacal
Movement of fur,
And the curded sound
Of your inward purr?
Where did he find
The gloomy, sunny
Spheres of your eyes,
Like globules of honey?
Under the velvet
Fall of your paws
Needles the light of your
Polished claws ...
Were you a Favorite,
Ages ago,
Who purred at an Emperor's
Overthrow?

Martha Ostenso
(1900-1963)

Cats

Cats, no less liquid than their shadows,
Offer no angles to the wind.
They slip, diminished, neat, through loopholes
Less than themselves; will not be pinned

To rules or routes for journeys; counter
Attack with non-resistance; twist
Enticing through the curving fingers
And leave an angered, empty fist.

They wait obsequious as darkness
Quick to retire, quick to return;
Admit no aim or ethics; flatter
With reservations; will not learn

To answer to their names; are seldom
Truly owned till shot or skinned.
Cats, no less liquid than their shadows,
Offer no angles to the wind.

A. S. J. Tessimond
(1902-1962)

The Cat

Dear creature by the fire a-purr,
   Strange idol eminently bland,
Miraculous puss! As o'er your fur
   I trail a negligible hand,

And gaze into your gazing eyes,
   And wonder in a demi-dream
What mystery it is that lies
   Behind those slits that glare and gleam,

An exquisite enchantment falls
   About the portals of my sense;
Meandering through enormous halls
   I breathe luxurious frankincense,

An ampler air, a warmer June
   Enfold me, and my wondering eye
Salutes a more imperial moon
   Throned in a more resplendent sky

Than ever knew this northern shore.
   O, strange! For you are with me too,
And I who am a cat once more
   Follow the woman that was you.

With tail erect and pompous march,
   The proudest puss that ever trod,
Through many a grove, 'neath many an arch,
   Impenetrable as a god,

Down many an alabaster flight
   Of broad and cedar-shaded stairs,
While over us the elaborate night
   Mysteriously gleams and glares!
            Lytton Strachey
            (1880-1932)

The Cat and the Moon

The cat went here and there
And the moon spun round like a top,
And the nearest kin of the moon,
The creeping cat, looked up.
Black Minnaloushe stared at the moon,
For, wander and wail as he would,
The pure cold light in the sky
Troubled his animal blood.
Minnaloushe runs in the grass
Lifting his delicate feet.
Do you dance, Minnaloushe, do you dance?
When two close kindred meet,
What better than call a dance?
Maybe the moon may learn,
Tired of that courtly fashion,
A new dance turn.
Minnaloushe creeps through the grass
From moonlit place to place,
The sacred moon overhead
Has taken a new phase.
Does Minnaloushe know that his pupils
Will pass from change to change,
And that from round to crescent,
From crescent to round they range?
Minnaloushe creeps through the grass
Alone, important and wise,
And lifts to the changing moon
His changing eyes.

William Butler Yeats
(1865-1939)

Cat Jeoffry

For I will consider my Cat Jeoffry.

For he is the servant of the Living God, duly and daily serving him.

For at the first glance of the glory of God in the East he worships in his way.

For this is done by wreathing his body seven times round with elegant quickness.

For then he leaps up to catch the musk, which is the blessing of God upon his prayer.

For he rolls upon prank to work it in.

For having done duty and received blessing he begins to consider himself.

For this he performs in ten degrees.

For first he looks upon his fore-paws to see if they are clean.

For secondly he kicks up behind to clear away there.

For thirdly he works it upon stretch with the fore-paws extended.

For fourthly he sharpens his paws with wood.

For fifthly he washes himself.

For sixthly he rolls upon wash.

For seventhly he fleas himself, that he may not be interrupted upon the beat.

For eighthly he rubs himself against a post.

For ninthly he looks up for his instructions.

For tenthly he goes in quest of food.

For having consider'd God and himself he will consider his neighbour.

For if he meets another cat he will kiss her in kindness.

For when he takes his prey he plays with it to give it a chance.

For one mouse in seven escapes by his dallying.

For when his day's work is done his business more properly begins.

For he keeps the Lord's watch in the night against the adversary.

For he counteracts the powers of darkness by his electrical skin and glaring eyes.

For he counteracts the Devil, who is death, by brisking about the life.

For in the morning orisons he loves the sun and the sun loves him.

For he is of the tribe of Tiger.

For the Cherub Cat is a term of the Angel Tiger.

For he has the subtlety and hissing of a serpent, which in goodness he suppresses.

For he will not do destruction, if he is well-fed, neither will he spit without provocation.

For he purrs in thankfulness, when God tells him he's a good Cat.

For he is an instrument for the children to learn benevolence upon.

For every house is incompleat without him and a blessing is lacking in the spirit.

For the Lord commanded Moses concerning the cats at the departure of the Children of Israel from Egypt.

For every family had one cat at least in the bag.

For the English Cats are the best in Europe.

For he is the cleanest in the use of his forepaws of any quadrupede.

For the dexterity of his defense is an instance of the love of God to him
exceedingly.

For he is the quickest to his mark of any creature.

For he is tenacious of his point.

For he is a mixture of gravity and waggery.

For he knows that God is his Saviour.

For there is nothing sweeter than his peace when at rest.

For there is nothing brisker than his life when in motion.

For he is of the Lord's poor, and so indeed is he called by benevolence
perpetually — Poor Jeoffry! poor Jeoffry! the rat has bit thy throat.

For I bless the name of the Lord Jesus that Jeoffry is better.

For the divine spirit comes about his body to sustain it in compleat cat.

For his tongue is exceeding pure so that it has in purity what it wants
in musick.

For he is docile and can learn certain things.

For he can set up with gravity which is patience upon approbation.

For he can fetch and carry, which is patience in employment.

For he can jump over a stick which is patience upon proof positive.

For he can spraggle upon waggle at the word of command.

For he can jump from an eminence into his master's bosom.

For he can catch the cork and toss it again.

For he is hated by the hypocrite and miser.

For the former is afraid of detection.

For the latter refuses the charge.

For he camels his back to bear the first motion of business.

For he is good to think on, if a man would express himself neatly.

For he made a great figure in Egypt for his signal services.

For he killed the Icneumon-rat very pernicious by land.

For his ears are so acute that they sting again.

For from this proceeds the passing quickness of his attention.

For by stroking of him I have found out electricity.

For I perceived God's light about him both wax and fire.

For the electrical fire is the spiritual substance, which God sends from
heaven to sustain the bodies both of man and beast.

For God has blessed him in the variety of his movements.

For, tho' he cannot fly, he is an excellent clamberer.

For his motions upon the face of the earth are more than any other
quadrupede.

For he can tread to all the measures upon the musick.

For he can swim for life.

For he can creep.

Christopher Smart
(1722-1771)

Cats

Passionate enthusiasts and scholars austere
Love equally, in their ripe season,
The powerful, gentle cats, pride of the home,
Who like their masters are heat seeking,
   and like them, sedentary.

Lovers of purity and of pleasure,
They seek out silence and the horror of shadows;
Erebus would have used them for funeral coursers,
Were they able to bend their dignity to servitude.

In meditation they take the noble attitudes
Of great sphinxes stretched in profound solitudes,
Who seem to sleep in a dream without end;

Their fertile loins crackle with sparkling magic,
And particles of gold, like fine sand,
Hazily star their mystical eyes.

Charles Baudelaire
(1821-1867)
translated from the French
by Dorothy Foster

To a cat

Stately, kindly, lordly friend
                    Condescend
Here to sit by me, and turn
Glorious eyes that smile and burn,
Golden eyes, love's lustrous meed,
On the golden page I read.

All your wondrous wealth of hair
                    Dark and fair,
Silken-shaggy, soft and bright
As the clouds and beams of night,
Pays my reverent hand's caress
Back with friendlier gentleness.

Dogs may fawn on all and some
                    As they come;
You, a friend of loftier mind,
Answers friends alone in kind.
Just your foot upon my hand
Softly bids it understand.
                    A. C. Swinburne
                    (1837-1909)

Cats and Kings

With wide unblinking stare
   The cat looked; but she did not see the king.
She only saw a two-legg'd creature there
   Who in due time might have tit-bits to fling.

The king was on his throne.
   In his left hand he grasped the golden ball.
She looked at him with eyes of bright green stone
   And thought, *what fun if he should let it fall.*

With swishing tail she lay
   And watched for happy accidents, while he,
The essential king, was brooding far away
   In his own world of hope and memory.

O, cats are subtle now,
   And kings are mice to many a modern mind;
And yet there throbbed behind that human brow
   The strangely simple thoughts that serve mankind.

The gulf might not be wide;
   But over it, at least, no cat could spring.
So once again an ancient adage lied.
   The cat looked; but she never saw the king.

                Alfred Noyes
                (1880-1958)

Fog

The fog comes
on little cat feet.

It sits looking
over harbor and city
on silent haunches
and then moves on.
            Carl Sandburg
            (1878-1967)

Unlost

    Her eyes run;
    Her feet see.
Hidden in smog,
Cat hurries home.
        Oliver Ingersoll
        (1912-   )

The Mysterious Cat

(A chant for children's pantomime dance,
suggested by a picture painted by George
Mather Richards)

I saw a proud, mysterious cat,
I saw a proud, mysterious cat,
Too proud to catch a mouse or rat —
Mew, mew, mew.

But catnip she would eat, and purr,
But catnip, she would eat, and purr.
And goldfish she did much prefer —
Mew, mew, mew.

I saw a cat — 'twas but a dream,
I saw a cat — 'twas but a dream
Who scorned the slave that brought her cream —
Mew, mew, mew.

Unless the slave were dressed in style,
Unless the slave were dressed in style,
And knelt before her all the while —
Mew, mew, mew.

Did you ever hear of a thing like that?
Did you ever hear of a thing like that?
Did you ever hear of a thing like that?
Oh, what a proud mysterious cat.
Oh, what a proud mysterious cat.
Oh, what a proud mysterious cat.
Mew . . . mew . . . mew.

*Vachel Lindsay
(1879-1931)*

The
Hungry Cat

Milk for the Cat

When the tea is brought at five o'clock,
And all the neat curtains are drawn with care,
The little black cat with bright green eyes
Is suddenly purring there.

At first she pretends, having nothing to do,
She has come in merely to blink by the grate,
But though tea may be late or the milk may be sour,
She is never late.

And presently her agate eyes
Take a soft large milky haze,
And her independent casual glance
Becomes a stiff, hard gaze.

Then she stamps her claws or lifts her ears
Or twists her tail and begins to stir,
Till suddenly all her little body becomes
One breathing, trembling purr.

The children eat and wriggle and laugh;
The two old ladies stroke their silk:
But the cat is grown small and thin with desire,
Transformed to a creeping lust for milk.

The white saucer like some full moon descends
At last from the cloud of the table above;
She sighs and dreams and thrills and glows,
Transfigured with love.

She nestles over the shining rim,
Buries her chin in the creamy sea;
Her tail hangs loose; each drowsy paw
Is doubled under each bending knee.

A long dim ecstasy holds her life;
Her world is an infinite shapeless white,
Till her tongue has curled the last holy drop;
Then she sinks back into the night,

Draws and dips her body to heap
Her sleepy nerves in the great arm-chair,
Lies defeated and buried deep
Three or four hours unconscious there.

Harold Monro
(1879-1932)

On Lutestrings Catt-Eaten

Are these the strings that poets feigne
Have clear'd the Ayre, and clam'd the mayne?
Charm'd wolves, and from the mountaine creasts
Made forests dance with all their beasts?
Could these neglected shreads you see
Inspire a Lute of Ivorie
And make it speake? Oh! think then what
Hath beene committed by my catt,
Who, in the silence of this night
Hath gnawne these cords, and marr'd them quite;
Leaving such reliques as may be
For fretts, not for my lute, but me.
Pusse, I will curse thee; may'st thou dwell
With some dry Hermit in a cell
Where Ratt neere peep'd, where mouse neere fedd,
And flyes goe supperlesse to bedd;
Or with some close-par'd Brother, where
Thou'lt fast each Saboath in the yeare;
Or else, prophane, be hang'd on Munday,
For butchering a mouse on Sunday;
Or May'st thou tumble from some tower,
And misse to light upon all fower,
Taking a fall that may untie
Eight of nine lives, and let them flye;
Or may the midnight embers sindge
Thy daintie coate, or Jane beswinge
Thy hide, when she shall take thee biting
Her cheese clouts, or her house beshiting.
What, was there neere a ratt nor mouse,
Nor Buttery ope? nought in the house
But harmlesse Lutestrings could suffice
Thy paunch, and draw thy glaring eyes?
Did not thy conscious stomach finde
Nature prophan'd, that kind with kind
Should staunch his hunger? thinke on that,
Thou caniball, and Cyclops catt.
For know, thou wretch, that every string
Is a catt-gutt, which art doth spinne
Into a thread; and how suppose
Dunstan, that snuff'd the divell's nose,
Should bid these strings revive, as once
He did the calfe, from naked bones;

Or I, to plague thee for thy sinne,
Should draw a circle, and beginne
To conjure, for I am, look to't,
An Oxford scholler, and can doo't.
Then with three setts of mopps and mowes,
Seaven of odd words, and motley showes,
A thousand tricks, that may be taken
From Faustus, Lambe, or Fryar Bacon:
I should beginne to call my strings
My catlings, and my mynikins;
And they recalled, straight should fall
To mew, to purr, to catterwaule
From puss's belly. Sure as death,
Pusse should be an Engastranith;
Pusse should be sent for to the king
For a strange bird, or some rare thing.
Pusse should be sought to farre and neere,
As she some cunning woman were.
Pusse should be carried up and downe,
From shire to shire, from Towne to Towne,
Like to the camell, Leane as Hagg,
The Elephant, or Apish nagg,
For a strange sight; pusse should be sung
In Lousy Ballads, midst the Throng
At markets, with as good a grace
As Agincourt, or Chevy-chase.
The Troy-sprung Brittan would forgoe
His pedigree he chaunteth soe,
And singe that Merlin — long deceast —
Returned is in a nyne-liv'd beast.
    Thus, pusse, thou seest what might betyde thee;
But I forbeare to hurt or chide thee;
For may be pusse was melancholy
And so to make her blythe and jolly,
Finding these strings, shee'ld have a fitt
Of mirth; nay, pusse, if that were it,
Thus I revenge mee, that as thou
Hast played on them, I've plaid on you;
And as thy touch was nothing fine,
Soe I've but scratch'd these notes of mine.

Thomas Master
(1603-1643)

Hungry Master and Hungry Cat

When my house was bare of skins and pots of meal,
after it had been inhabited, not empty, full of folk and richly
    prosperous,
I see the mice avoid my house, retiring to the governor's palace.
The flies have called for a move, whether their wings are clipped
    or whole.
The cat stayed a year in the house and did not see a mouse
shaking its head at hunger, at a life full of pain and spite.
When I saw the pained downcast head, the heat in the belly, I
    said,
"Patience; you are the best cat my eyes ever saw in a ward."
He said, "I have no patience. How can I stay in a desert like
    the belly of a she ass?"
I said, "Go in peace to a hotel where travellers are many and
    much trade,
Even if the spider spins in my wine jar, in the jug, and the pot."
Abu Shamaqmaq
(c. 770)
translated from the Arabic
by Dr. A. S. Tritton

The Cat and the Partridge

Your master grieved as though you'd savaged *him*,
When you devoured his partridge, wicked cat.
The hounds which tore Actaeon limb from limb,
Fierce man-eaters, did hardly worse than that.
And now so set on patridge is your soul,
The mice can dance and rob your dainty bowl.
Damocharis the Grammarian
(c. 550)
translated from the Greek
by W. Bedell Stanford

Fable XXI
The Rat-Catcher and Cats

The rats by night such mischief did,
Betty was ev'ry morning chid.
They undermined whole sides of bacon,
Her cheese was sapp'd, her tarts were taken.
Her pasties, fenced with thickest paste,
Were all demolish'd, and laid waste.
She cursed the Cat for want of duty,
Who left her foes a constant booty.

 An engineer, of noted skill,
Engaged to stop the growing ill.

 From room to room he now surveys
Their haunts, their works, their secret ways;
Finds where they 'scape an ambuscade,
And whence the nightly sally's made,

 An envious Cat from place to place,
Unseen, attends his silent pace.
She saw that if his trade went on,
The purring race must be undone;
So, secretly removes his baits,
And ev'ry stratagem defeats.

 Again he sets the poison'd toils,
And Puss again the labour foils.

 What foe (to frustrate my designs)
My schemes thus nightly countermines?
Incensed, he cries, this very hour
The wretch shall bleed beneath my power.

 So said, a pond'rous trap he brought,
And in the fact poor Puss was caught.

 Smuggler, says he, thou shalt be made
A victim to our loss of trade.

 The captive Cat, with piteous mews,
For pardon, life, and freedom sues.
A sister of the science spare;
One int'rest is our common care.

 What insolence! the man replied;
Shall Cats with us the game divide?
Were all your interloping band
Extinquish'd, or expell'd the land,
We Rat-catchers might raise our fees,
Sole guardians of a nation's cheese!

A Cat, who saw the lifted knife,
Thus spoke, and saved her sister's life:
   In ev'ry age and clime we see,
Two of a trade can ne'er agree.
Each hates his neighbour for encroaching;
'Squire stigmatizes 'squire for poaching;
Beauties with beauties are in arms,
And scandal pelts each other's charms;
Kings, too, their neighbour kings dethrone,
In hope to make the world their own.
But let us limit our desires,
Not war like beauties, kings, and 'squires!
For though we both one prey pursue,
There's game enough for us and you.

John Gay
(1685-1732)

To Mrs. Reynolds' Cat

Cat! who hast pass'd thy grand climacteric,
    How many mice and rats hast in thy days
    Destroyed? — How many titbits stolen? Gaze
With those bright languid segments green, and prick
Those velvet ears — but pr'ythee do not stick
    Thy latent talons in me — and upraise
    Thy gentle mew — and tell me all thy frays,
Of fish and mice, and rats and tender chick.
Nay, look not down, nor lick thy dainty wrists —
    For all thy wheezy asthma, — and for all
Thy tail's tip is nick'd off — and though the fists
    Of many a maid have given thee many a maul,
Still is that fur as soft as when the lists
    In youth thou enter'dst on glass-bottled wall.

John Keats
(1795-1821)

The Mournful Chirping

Eaten by the cat!
  Perhaps the cricket's widow
  may be bewailing that!
        Kikaku
       (1661-1707)

The
Hunter

The Prize Cat

Pure blood domestic, guaranteed,
Soft-mannered, musical in purr,
The ribbon had declared the breed,
Gentility was in the fur.

Such feline culture in the gads
No anger ever arched her back —
What distance since those velvet pads
Departed from the leopard's track!

And when I mused how Time had thinned
The jungle strains within the cells,
How human hands had disciplined
Those prowling optic parallels;

I saw the generations pass
Along the reflex of a spring,
A bird had rustled in the grass,
The tab had caught it on the wing:

Behind the leap so furtive-wild
Was such ignition in the gleam,
I thought an Abyssinian child
Had cried out in the whitethroat's scream.

                    E. J. Pratt
                    (1882-1964)

A Cat

She had a name among the children;
But no one loved though someone owned
Her, locked her out of doors at bedtime
And had her kittens duly drowned.

In Spring, nevertheless, this cat
Ate blackbirds, thrushes, nightingales,
And birds of bright voice and plume and flight,
As well as scraps from neighbours' pails.

I loathed and hated her for this;
One speckle on a thrush's breast
Was worth a million such; and yet
She lived long, till God gave her rest.

Edward Thomas
(1878-1917)

The Old Cat and the Young Mouse

A young mouse, with little experience,
Tried to sway an old cat by crying for clemence,
And pleading the mercy of Raminagrobis:
> "Let me live. I'm quite wee.
> Is my nourishment a consequence
> To anyone but me?
> Have the master and his family
> Starved because I ate?
> I'm stuffed with one pea.
> One nut fills my plate.
Now I am skinny; but bide your time, stay my sentence.
Fatten me up for your descendants."
Thus appealed the entrapped mouse to the old cat.
The cat replied: "You deceive yourself to think like that.
To whom do you think you address your speaking?
I have deaf ears for your shrieking and squeaking.
Talking never stopped wars. Don't expect mercy from
   old soldiers.
> Obey Nature's demand.
> Die! And at my hand!
> Argue your fate with the Spinning Sisters.
My children don't need their menus planned."
> So much for words. And as for my fable,
Here is the moral sense it does contain:

Youth is too self-assured, arrogant, vain.
> Old age is ruthless and inflexible.

Jean de La Fontaine
(1621-1695)
translated from the French
by Dorothy Foster

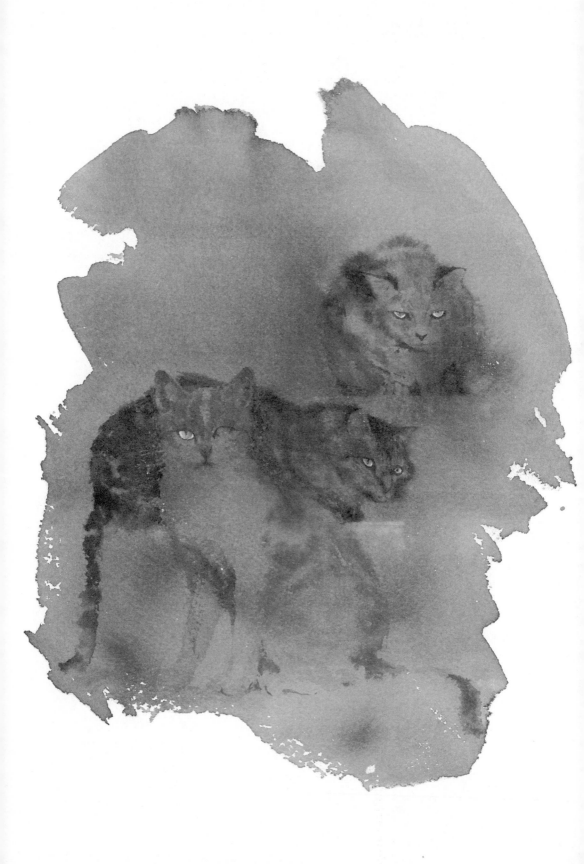

Five Eyes

In Hans' old Mill his three black cats
Watch his bins for thieving rats
Whisker and claw, they crouch in the night,
Their five eyes smouldering green and bright:
Squeaks from the flour sacks, squeaks from where
The cold wind stirs on the empty stair,
Squeaking and scampering, everywhere.
Then down they pounce, now in, now out,
At whisking tail, and sniffing snout;
While lean old Hans he snores away
Till peep of light at break of day;
Then up he climbs to his creaking mill,
Out come his cats all grey with meal —
Jekkel, and Jessup, and one-eyed Jill.

Walter de la Mare
(1873-1956)

To a Cat, Killed as she was robbing a Dove-cote

Poor Puss is gone! 'Tis fate's decree —
Yet I must still her loss deplore,
For dearer than a child was she,
And ne'er shall I behold her more.

With many a sad presaging tear
This morn I saw her steal away,
While she went on without a fear
Except that she should miss her prey.

I saw her to the dove-house climb,
With cautious feet and slow she stept,
Resolved to balance loss of time
By eating faster than she crept.

Her subtle foes were on the watch
And mark'd her course, with fury fraught,
And while she hoped the birds to catch,
An arrow's point the huntress caught.

In fancy she had got them all,
And drunk their blood, and suck'd their breath;
Alas! she only got a fall,
And only drank the draught of death.

Why, why was pigeons' flesh so nice,
That thoughtless cats should love it thus?
Hadst thou but lived on rats and mice,
Thou hadst been living still, poor Puss.

Curst be the taste, howe'er refined,
That prompts us for such joys to wish,
And curst the dainty where we find
Destruction lurking in the dish.

> *Ibn Alalaf Alnaharwany*
> *(c. 889)*
> *translated from the Arabic*
> *by J. D. Carlyle*

The
Curious Cat

Cat, Cat

Cat, cat, he wears a hat,
Jumps on high for this and that.

Cat, cat, the curious one,
Finds the wool before you're done.

Cat, cat, so bright and sharp,
Then feel his claw in one quick arc.

Cat, cat, the nine-lives treat,
Whose antics make you laugh and weep.

Cat, cat, who makes your day
The cat you love - Or so you say!

Anonymous

Poem

As the cat
climbed over
the top of

the jamcloset
first the right
forefoot

carefully
then the hind
stepped down

into the pit of
the empty
flowerpot.
  William Carlos Williams
  (1883-1963)

The Retired Cat

A poet's cat, sedate and grave,
As poet well could wish to have,
Was much addicted to inquire
For nooks to which she might retire,
And where, secure as mouse in chink,
She might repose, or sit and think.
I know not where she caught the trick —
Nature perhaps herself had cast her
In such a mould *philosophique*,
Or else she learn'd it of her master.
Sometimes ascending, debonair,
An apple tree or lofty pear,
Lodg'd with convenience in the fork,
She watched the gard'ner at his work;
Sometimes her ease and solace sought
In an old empty wat'ring pot,
There wanting nothing, save a fan,
Tc seem some nymph in her sedan,
Apparell'd in exactest sort,
And ready to be borne to court.

But love of change it seems has place
Not only in our wiser race;
Cats also feel as well as we
That Passion's force, and so did she.
Her climbing, she began to find,
Expos'd her too much to the wind,
And the old utensil of tin
Was cold and comfortless within:
She therefore wish'd instead of those,
Some place of more serene repose,
Where neither cold might come, nor air
Too rudely wanton with her hair,
And sought it in the likeliest mode
Within her master's snug abode.

A draw'r, — it chanc'd, at bottom lin'd
With linen of the softest kind,
With such as merchants introduce
From India, for the ladies' use, —
A draw'r impending o'er the rest,
Half open in the topmost chest,
Of depth enough, and none to spare,
Invited her to slumber there.

Puss, with delight beyond expression,
Survey'd the scene, and took possession.
Recumbent at her ease ere long,
And lull'd by her own humdrum song,
She left the cares of life behind,
And slept as she would sleep her last,
When in came, housewifely inclin'd,
The chambermaid, and shut it fast,
By no malignity impell'd,
But all unconscious whom it held.

Awaken'd by the shock (cried puss)
Was ever cat attended thus!
The open draw'r was left, I see,
Merely to prove a nest for me,
For soon as I was well compos'd,
Then came the maid, and it was closed:
How smooth these 'kerchiefs, and how sweet.
O what a delicate retreat!
I will resign myself to rest
Till Sol, declining in the west,
Shall call to supper; when, no doubt,
Susan will come and let me out.

The evening came, the sun descended,
And puss remain'd still unattended.
The night roll'd tardily away
(With her indeed 'twas never day),
The sprightly morn her course renew'd,
The evening grey again ensued.
And puss came into mind no more
Than if entomb'd the day before.
With hunger pinch'd, and pinch'd for room,
She now presag'd approaching doom,
Nor slept a single wink, or purr'd,
Conscious of jeopardy incurr'd.

That night, by chance, the poet, watching,
Heard an inexplicable scratching,
His noble heart went pit-a-pat,
And to himself he said — what's that?
He drew the curtain at his side,
And forth he peep'd, but nothing spied.

Yet, by his ear direct'd, guess'd
Something imprison'd in the chest,
And doubtful what, with prudent care,
Resolv'd it should continue there.
At length a voice, which well he knew,
A long and melancholy mew,
Saluting his poetic ears,
Consol'd him, and dispell'd his fears;
He left his bed, he trod the floor,
He 'gan in haste the draw'rs explore,
The lowest first, and without stop,
The rest in order to the top.
For 'tis a truth well known to most,
That whatsoever thing is lost,
We seek it, ere it come to light,
In ev'ry cranny but the right.
Forth skipp'd the cat; not now replete
As erst with airy self-conceit,
Nor in her own fond apprehension,
A theme for all the world's attention,
But modest, sober, cur'd of all
Her notions hyberbolical,
And wishing for a place of rest
Anything rather than a chest:
Then stept the poet into bed,
With this reflexion in his head:

Moral

Beware of too sublime a sense
Of your own worth and consequence!
The man who dreams himself so great
And his importance of such weight,
That all around, in all that's done,
Must move and act for him alone,
Will learn, in school of tribulation,
The folly of his expectation.
                    William Cowper
                    (1731-1800)

The Kitten

The Kitten

Always it's pouncing at nothing
Striking with both paws at once.
Although there is nothing to see
It seems that the kitten sees something
Or that he's compelled to exert
Such force as he is supplied with,
Must exert it, practise it
Even on nothing at all.
The attraction of nothing at all?
Imagination, maybe —
Present even in kittens —
Dim in the small kitten brain;
A mousetail flickering past
Just beyond reach of his claws
Perhaps, or a ball of yarn
To be rolled to and fro on the floor.
Such force as he is supplied with
Must be exerted it seems,
And what beyond this is the ultimate
The divine purpose of cats?

W. W. E. Ross
(1894-1966)

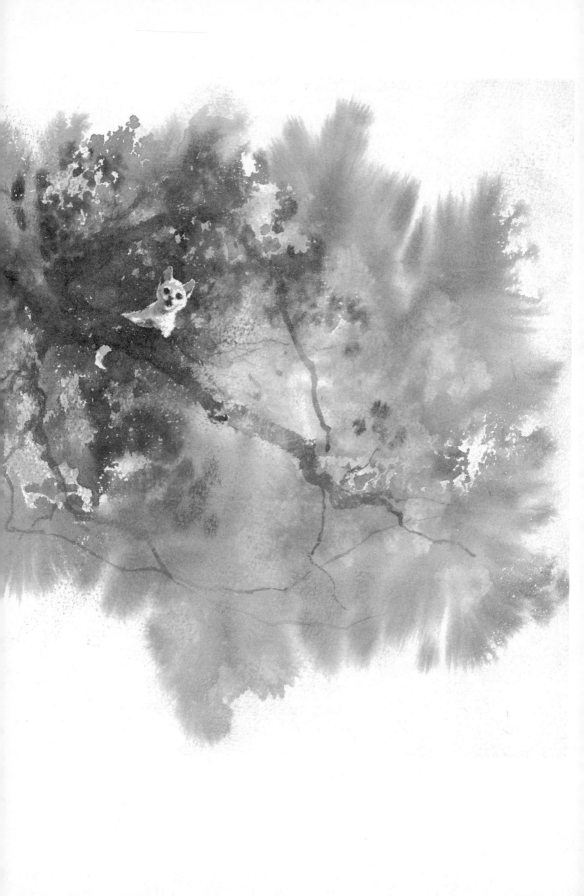

The Happy Cat

The cat's asleep; I whisper *kitten*
Till he stirs a little and begins to purr —
He doesn't wake. Today out on the limb
(The limb he thinks he can't climb down from)
He mewed until I heard him in the house.
I climbed up to get him down: he mewed.
What he says and what he sees are limited.
My own response is even more constricted.
I think, "It's lucky; what you have is too."
What do you have except — well, me?
I joke about it but it's not a joke:
The house and I are all he remembers.
Next month how will he guess that it is winter
And not just entropy, the universe
Plunging at last into its cold decline?
I cannot think of him without a pang.
Poor rumpled thing, why don't you see
That you have no more, really, than a man?
Men aren't happy: why are you?

                              Randall Jarrell
                              (1914-1965)

The Kitten and Falling Leaves

That way look, my Infant, lo!
What a pretty baby-show!
See the Kitten on the wall,
Sporting with the leaves that fall,
Withered leaves — one — two — and three —
From the lofty elder-tree!
Through the calm and frosty air
Of this morning bright and fair,
Eddying round and round they sink
Softly, slowly: one might think,
From the motions that are made,
Every little leaf conveyed
Sylph or Faery hither tending, —
To this lower world descending,
Each invisible and mute,
In his wavering parachute.
— But the Kitten, how she starts,
Crouches, stretches, paws, and darts!
First at one, and then its fellow,
Just as light and just as yellow;
There are many now — now one —
Now they stop and there are none:
What intenseness of desire
In her upward eye of fire!
With a tiger-leap half-way
Now she meets the coming prey,
Lets it go as fast, and then
Has it in her power again:
Now she works with three or four
Like an Indian conjurer;
Quick as he in feats of art,
Far beyond in joy of heart.
Were her antics played in the eye
Of a thousand standers-by,
Clapping hands with shout and stare,
What would little Tabby care
For the plaudits of the crowd?
Over happy to be proud,
Over wealthy in the treasure
Of her own exceeding pleasure!

'Tis a pretty baby-treat;
Nor, I deem, for me unmeet;
Here, for neither Babe nor me,
Other playmate can I see.

Of the countless living things,
That with stir of feet and wings
(In the sun or under shade,
Upon bough or grassy blade)
And with busy revellings,
Chirp and song, and murmurings,
Made this orchard's narrow space,
And this vale, so blithe a place;
Multitudes are swept away
Never more to breathe the day:
Some are sleeping; some in bands
Travelled into distant lands;
Others slunk to moor and wood,
Far from human neighbourhood;
And, among the Kinds that keep
With us closer fellowship,
With us openly abide,
All have laid their mirth aside.

   Where is he, that giddy Sprite,
Blue-cap, with his colours bright,
Who was blest as bird could be,
Feeding in the apple-tree;
Made such wanton spoil and rout,
Turning blossoms inside out:
Hung — head pointing towards the ground —
Fluttered, perched, into a round
Bound himself, and then unbound;
Lithest, gaudiest Harlequin!
Prettiest Tumbler ever seen!
Light of heart and light of limb;
What is now become of Him?
Lambs, that through the mountains went
Frisking, bleating merriment,
When the year was in its prime,
They are sobered by this time.
If you look to vale or hill,
If you listen, all is still,
Save a little neighbouring rill,
That from out the rocky ground
Strikes a solitary sound.
Vainly glitter hill and plain,
And the air is calm in vain;
Vainly Morning spreads the lure
Of a sky serene and pure;

Creature none can she decoy
Into open sign of joy:
Is it that they have a fear
Of the dreary season near?
Or that other pleasures be
Sweeter even than gaiety?

Yet, whate'er enjoyments dwell
In the impenetrable cell
Of the silent heart which Nature
Furnishes to every creature;
Whatsoe'er we feel and know
Too sedate for outward show,
Such a light of gladness breaks,
Pretty Kitten! from thy freaks, —
Spreads with such a living grace
O'er my little Dora's face;
Yes, the sight so stirs and charms
Thee, Baby, laughing in my arms,
That almost I could repine
That your transports are not mine,
That I do not wholly fare
Even as ye do, thoughtless pair!
And I will have my careless season
Spite of melancholy reason,
Will walk through life in such a way
That, when time brings on decay,
Now and then I may possess
Hours of perfect gladsomeness.
— Pleased by any random toy:
By a kitten's busy joy,
Or an infant's laughing eye
Sharing in the ecstasy;
I would fare like that or this,
Find my wisdom in my bliss;
Keep the sprightly soul awake,
And have faculties to take,
Even from things by sorrow wrought,
Matter for a jocund thought,
Spite of care, and spite of grief,
To gambol with Life's falling Leaf.

William Wordsworth
(1770-1850)

A Dirge for a Righteous Kitten

(To be intoned, all but the two italicized
lines, which are to be spoken in a snappy
matter-of-fact way)

Ding-dong, ding-dong, ding-dong.
Here lies a kitten good, who kept
A kitten's proper place.
He stole no pantry eatables,
Nor scratched the baby's face.
He let the alley-cats alone.
He had no yowling vice.
His shirt was always laundried well,
He freed the house of mice.
Until his death he had not caused
His little mistress tears,
He wore his ribbon prettily,
He washed behind his ears.
Ding-dong, ding-dong, ding-dong.
Vachel Lindsay
(1879-1931)

The Kitten

Wanton droll, whose harmless play
Beguiles the rustic's closing day,
When, drawn the evening fire about,
Sit aged crone and thoughtless lout,
And child upon his three-foot stool,
Waiting until his supper cool,
And maid, whose cheek outblooms the rose,
As bright the blazing faggot glows,
Who bending to the friendly light,
Plies her task with busy sleight;
Come, show thy tricks and sportive graces,
Thus circled round with merry faces!
Backward coil'd and crouching low,
With glaring eyeballs watch thy foe,
The housewife's spindle whirling round,
Or thread, or straw, that on the ground
Its shadow throws, by urchin sly
Held out to lure thy roving eye;
Then stealing onward, fiercely spring
Upon the tempting, faithless thing.
Now whirling round with bootless skill,
Thy bo-peep tail provokes thee still,
As still beyond thy curving side
Its jetty tip is seen to glide;
Till from thy centre starting far,
Thou sidelong veer'st with rump in air
Erected stiff, and gait awry,
Like madam in her tantrums high;
Though ne'er a madam of them all,
Whose silken kirtle sweeps the hall,
More varied trick and whim displays
To catch the admiring stranger's gaze.
Doth power in measured verses dwell,
All thy vagaries wild to tell?
Ah, no! the start, the jet, the bound,
The giddy scamper round and round,
With leap and toss and high curvet,
And many a whirling somerset
(Permitted by the modern Muse
Expression technical to use),
These mock the deftest rhymester's skill,
But poor in art, though rich in will.

The featest tumbler, stage bedight,
To thee is but a clumsy wight,
Who every limb and sinew strains
To do what costs thee little pains;
For which, I trow, the gaping crowd
Requites him oft with plaudits loud.
But, stopp'd the while thy wanton play,
Applauses too thy pains repay:
For then beneath some urchin's hand
With modest pride thou tak'st thy stand,
While many a stroke of kindness glides
Along thy back and tabby sides.
Dilated swells thy glossy fur,
And loudly croons thy busy purr,
As, timing well the equal sound,
Thy clutching feet bepat the ground,
And all their harmless claws disclose
Like prickles of an early rose,
While softly from thy whisker'd cheek
Thy half-closed eyes peer, mild and meek.
But not alone by cottage fire
Do rustics rude thy feats admire.
The learned sage, whose thoughts explore
The widest range of human lore,
Or with unfetter'd fancy fly
Through airy heights of poesy,
Pausing, smiles with alter'd air
To see thee climb his elbow-chair,
Or, struggling on the mat below,
Hold warfare with his slipper'd toe.
The widow'd dame, or lonely maid,
Who, in the still, but cheerless shade
Of home unsocial, spends her age,
And rarely turns a letter'd page,
Upon her hearth for thee lets fall
The rounded cork, or paper ball,
Nor chides thee on thy wicked watch,
The ends of ravell'd skein to catch,
But lets thee have thy wayward will,
Perplexing oft her better skill.
E'en he, whose mind of gloomy bent,
In lonely tower, or prison pent,
Reviews the coil of former days,

And loathes the world and all its ways;
What time the lamp's unsteady gleam
Hath roused him from his moody dream,
Feels, as thou gambol'st round his seat,
His heart of pride less fiercely beat,
And smiles, a link in thee to find,
That joins it still to living kind.
Whence hast thou then, thou witless puss,
The magic power to charm us thus?
Is it that in thy glaring eye
And rapid movements, we descry —
Whilst we at ease, secure from ill,
The chimney corner snugly fill —
A lion darting on his prey,
A tiger at his ruthless play?
Or, is it, that in thee we trace
With all thy varied wanton grace,
An emblem, view'd with kindred eye,
Of tricky, restless infancy?
Ah! many a lightly sportive child,
Who hath like thee our wits beguiled,
To dull and sober manhood grown,
With strange recoil our hearts disown.
Even so, poor kit! must thou endure,
When thou become'st a cat demure,
Full many a cuff and angry word,
Chid roughly from the tempting board,
And yet, for that thou hast, I ween,
So oft our favoured playmate been,
Soft be the change, which thou shalt prove,
When time hath spoiled thee of our love;
Still be thou deem'd, by housewife fat,
A comely, careful, mousing cat,
Whose dish is, for the public good,
Replenish'd oft with savoury food.
Nor, when thy span of life be past,
Be thou to pond or dunghill cast;
But gently borne on goodman's spade,
Beneath the decent sod be laid.
And children show, with glistening eyes,
The place where poor old Pussy lies.
                    Joanna Baillie
                    (1762-1851)

Ultra-pink peony...
Silver Siamese soft cat...
Gold-dust butterfly...
Buson
(1715-1783)

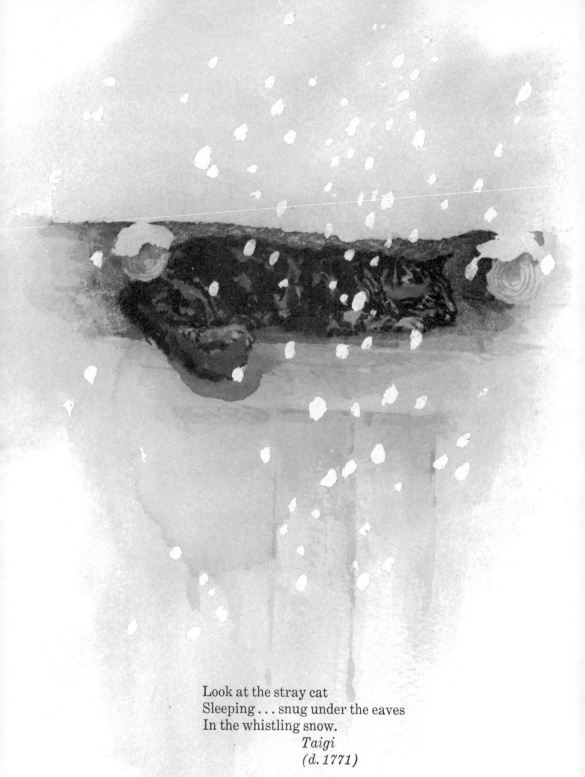

Look at the stray cat
Sleeping . . . snug under the eaves
In the whistling snow.
        Taigi
      (d. 1771)

Placing the kitten
To weigh her on the balance . . .
She went on playing.
Issa
(1763-1827)

Rainy afternoon . . .
Little daughter you will never
Teach that cat to dance.
Issa
(1763-1827)

Rhymes and Ballads

from *The Bad Child's Book of Beasts*

Introduction

I call you bad, my little child,
　　Upon the title page,
Because a manner rude and wild
　　Is common at your age.

The Moral of this priceless work
　　(If rightly understood)
Will make you — from a little Turk —
　　Unnaturally good.

Do not as evil children do,
　　Who on the slightest grounds
Will imitate the Kangaroo,
　　With wild unmeaning bounds.

Do not as children badly bred,
　　Who eat like little Hogs,
And when they have to go to bed
　　Will whine like Puppy Dogs:

Who take their manners from the Ape,
　　Their habits from the Bear,
Indulge the loud unseemly jape,
　　And never brush their hair.

But son, control your actions that
　　Your friends may all repeat,
'This Child is dainty as the Cat,
　　And as the Owl discreet.'

The Lion

The Lion, the Lion, he dwells in the waste,
He has a big head and a very small waist;
But his shoulders are stark, and his jaws they are grim,
And a good little child will not play with him.

The Tiger

The Tiger, on the other hand, is kittenish and mild,
He makes a pretty playfellow for any little child;
And mothers of large families (who claim to common sense)
Will find a Tiger will repay the trouble and expense.

Hilaire Belloc
(1870-1953)

I Like Little Pussy

I like little Pussy, her coat is so warm,
And if I don't hurt her she'll do me no harm;
So I'll not pull her tail, nor drive her away,
But Pussy and I very gently will play.
                              Mother Goose
                              (c. 1760)

Little Robin Redbreast Sat upon a Tree

Little Robin Redbreast sat upon a tree,
Up went the Pussy-cat, and down went he,
Down came Pussy-cat, away Robin ran;
Says little Robin Redbreast: "Catch me if you can!"

Little Robin Redbreast jumped upon a spade,
Pussy-cat jumped after him, and then he was afraid.
Little Robin chirped and sang, and what did Pussy say?
Pussy-cat said: "Mew, mew, mew," and Robin flew away.

Mother Goose
(c. 1760)

Pussy-cat Sits by the Fire

Pussy-cat sits by the fire;
 How can she be fair?
In walks the little dog;
 Says: "Pussy, are you there?
How do you do, Mistress Pussy?
 Mistress Pussy, how d'ye do?"
"I thank you kindly, little dog,
 I fare as well as you!"
     Mother Goose
     (c. 1760)

Pussy-Cat, Pussy-Cat

Pussy-cat, Pussy-cat, where have you been?
I've been to London to see the Queen.
Pussy-cat, Pussy-cat, what did you there?
I frightened a little mouse under the chair.
     Mother Goose
     (c. 1760)

Ding-Dong-Bell

Ding-dong-bell, the cat's in the well.
 Who put her in? Little Johnny Green.
 Who pulled her out? Great Johnny Stout.
  What a naughty boy was that
  To drown a poor pussy-cat
 Who never did him any harm,
 And killed the mice in his father's barn.
     Mother Goose
     (c. 1760)

Three Tabbies

Three tabbies took out their cats to tea,
As well-behaved tabbies as well could be:
Each sat in the chair that each preferred,
They mewed for their milk, and they sipped and purred.
Now tell me this (as these cats you've seen them) —
How many lives had these cats between them?

Kate Greenaway
(1846-1901)

Old Scots Nursery Rhyme

There was a wee bit mousikie,
    That lived in Gilberaty, O,
It couldna get a bite o' cheese,
    For cheetie-poussie-cattie, O.

It said unto the cheesikie,
    "Oh fain wad I be at ye, O,
If 't were na for the cruel paws
    O' cheetie-poussie-cattie, O."

Anonymous
(c. 1650)

The Owl and the Pussy-cat

The Owl and the Pussy-cat went to sea
   In a beautiful pea-green boat:
They took some honey, and plenty of money
   Wrapped up in a five-pound note.
The Owl looked up to the stars above,
   And sang to a small guitar,
"O lovely Pussy, O Pussy, my love,
   What a beautiful Pussy you are,
          You are,
          You are!
What a beautiful Pussy you are!"

Pussy said to the Owl, "You elegant fowl,
   How charmingly sweet you sing!
Oh! let us be married; too long we have tarried:
   But what shall we do for a ring?"
They sailed away, for a year and a day,
   To the land where the bong-tree grows;
And there in a wood a Piggy-wig stood,
   With a ring at the end of his nose,
          His nose,
          His nose,
With a ring at the end of his nose.

"Dear Pig, are you willing to sell for one shilling
   Your ring?" Said the Piggy, "I will."
So they took it away, and were married next day
   By the Turkey who lives on the hill.
They dined on mince and slices of quince,
   Which they ate with a runcible spoon;
And hand in hand, on the edge of the sand,
   They danced by the light of the moon,
          The moon,
          The moon,
They danced by the light of the moon.

Edward Lear
(1812-1888)

The Cat Sits at the Mill Door

The cat sits at the mill door spinnin', spinnin'.
Up comes a wee mouse rinnin', rinnin'.
"What are ye doin' there my lady, my lady?"
"Spinnin' a sark for my son," quo' Batty, quo' Batty.
"I'll tell a story, my lady, my lady."
"We'll hae the mair company," quo' Batty, quo' Batty.
"There was once a wee woman, my lady, my lady."
"She tuk the less room," quo' Batty, quo' Batty.
"She was sweepin' her hoose one day, my lady, my lady."
"She had it the cleaner," quo' Batty, quo' Batty.
"She found a penny, my lady, my lady."
"She had the mair money," quo' Batty, quo' Batty.
"She went to the market, my lady, my lady."
"She didna stay at hame," quo' Batty, quo' Batty.
"She bocht a wee bit o' beef, my lady, my lady."
"She had the mair flesh meet," quo' Batty, quo' Batty.
"She cam' home my lady, my lady."
"She didna stay awa'," quo' Batty, quo' Batty.
"She put her beef on the coals to roast, my lady, my lady."
"She didna eat it raw," quo' Batty, quo' Batty.
"She put it on the window to cool, my lady, my lady."
"She didna scaud her lips," quo' Batty, quo' Batty.
"Up comes a wee mouse an' ate it all up, my lady, my lady."
"Ay, and that's the way I'll eat *you* up too," quo' Batty, quo' Batty.

> Quo' Batty, quo' Batty,
> Quo' BATTY.
> > *Anonymous*
> > *(c. 1600)*

The
Tomcat

Puss-Puss!

—Oh, Auntie, isn't he a beauty! And is he a gentleman or a lady?
—Neither, my dear! I had him fixed. It saves him from so many
   undesirable associations.

D. H. Lawrence
(1885-1930)

mehitabel s extensive past

(by archy the cockroach)

mehitabel the cat claims that
she has a human soul
also and has transmigrated
from body to body and it
may be so boss you
remember i told you she accused
herself of being cleopatra once i
asked her about antony

anthony who she asked me are
you thinking of that
song about rowley and gammon and
spinach heigho for anthony rowley

no i said mark antony the
great roman the friend of
caesar surely cleopatra you
remember j caesar

listen archy she said i
have been so many different
people in my time and met
so many prominent gentlemen i
won t lie to you or stall i
do get my dates mixed sometimes
think of how much i have had a
chance to forget and i have
always made a point of not
carrying grudges over
from one life to the next archy

i have been
used something fierce in my time but
i am no bum sport archy
i am a free spirit archy i
look on myself as being
quite a romantic character oh the
queens i have been and the
swell feeds i have ate
a cockroach which you are
and a poet which you used to be
archy couldn t understand
my feelings at having come
down to this i have
had bids to elegant feeds where poets

and cockroaches would
neither one be mentioned without a
laugh archy i have had
adventures but i
have never been an adventuress
one life up and the next life
down archy but always a lady
through it all and a
good mixer too always the
life of the party archy but never
anything vulgar always free footed
archy never tied down to
a job or housework yes looking
back on it all i can say is
i had some romantic
lives and some elegant times i
have seen better days archy but
what s the use of kicking kid it s
all in the game like a gentleman
friend of mine used to say
toujours gai kid toujours gai he
was an elegant cat he used
to be a poet himself and he made up
some elegant poetry about me and him

let s hear it i said and
mehitabel recited

persian pussy from over the sea
demure and lazy and smug and fat
none of your ribbons and bells for me
ours is the zest of the alley cat
over the roofs from flat to flat
we prance with capers corybantic
what though a boot should break a slat
mehitabel us for the life romantic

we would rather be rowdy and gaunt and free
and dine on a diet of roach and rat

roach i said what do you
mean roach interrupting mehitabel
yes roach she said that s the
way my boy friend made it up
i climbed in amongst the typewriter
keys for she had an excited
look in her eyes go on mehitabel i

said feeling safer and she
resumed her elocution

we would rather be rowdy and gaunt and free
and dine on a diet of roach and rat
than slaves to a tame society
ours is the zest of the alley cat
fish heads freedom a frozen sprat
dug from the gutter with digits frantic
is better than bores and a fireside mat
mehitabel us for the life romantic

when the pendant moon in the leafless tree
clings and sways like a golden bat
i sing its light and my love for thee
ours is the zest of the alley cat
missiles around us fall rat a tat tat
but our shadows leap in a ribald antic
as over the fences the world cries scat
mehitabel us for the life romantic

persian princess i dont care that
for your pedigree traced by scribes pedantic
ours is the zest of the alley cat
mehitabel us for the life romantic

ain t that high brow stuff
archy i always remembered it
but he was an elegant gent
even if he was a highbrow and a
regular bohemian archy him and
me went aboard a canal boat
one day and he got his head into
a pitcher of cream and couldn t get
it out and fell overboard
he come up once before he
drowned toujours gai kid he
gurgled and then sank for ever that
was always his words archy toujours
gai kid toujours gai i
have known some swell gents
in my time dearie

Don Marquis
(1878-1937)

cheerio, my deario

(by archy the cockroach)

well boss i met
mehitabel the cat
trying to dig a
frozen lamb chop
out of a snow
drift the other day

a heluva comedown
that is for me archy
she says a few
brief centuries
ago one of old
king
tut
ankh
amen s favourite
queens and today
the village scavenger
but wotthehell
archy wotthehell
it s cheerio
my deario that
pulls a lady through

see here mehitabel
i said i thought
you told me that
it was cleopatra
you used to be
before you
transmigrated into
the carcase of a cat
where do you get
this tut
ankh
amen stuff
question mark

i was several
ladies my little
insect says she
being cleopatra was
only an incident
in my career

and i was always getting
the rough end of it
always being
misunderstood by some
strait laced
prune faced bunch
of prissy mouthed
sisters of uncharity
the things that
have been said
about me archy
exclamation point

and all simply
because i was a
live dame
the palaces i have
been kicked out of
in my time
exclamation point

but wotthehell
little archy wot
thehell
it s cheerio
my deario
that pulls a
lady through
exclamation point

framed archy always
framed that is the
story of all my lives
no chance for a dame
with the anvil chorus
if she shows a little
motion it seems to

me only yesterday
that the luxor local
number one of
the ladies axe
association got me in
dutch with king tut and
he slipped me the
sarcophagus always my
luck yesterday an empress
and today too
emaciated to interest
a vivisectionist but
toujours gai archy
toujours gai and always
a lady in spite of hell
and transmigration
once a queen
always a queen
archy
period

one of her
feet was frozen
but on the other three
she began to caper and
dance singing it s
cheerio my deario
that pulls a lady
through her morals may
have been mislaid somewhere
in the centuries boss but
i admire her spirit

archy
Don Marquis
(1878-1937)

The Tom-cat

At midnight in the alley
   A Tom-cat comes to wail,
And he chants the hate of a million years
   As he swings his snaky tail.

Malevolent, bony, brindled,
   Tiger and devil and bard,
His eyes are coals from the middle of Hell
   And his heart is black and hard.

He twists and crouches and capers
   And bares his curved sharp claws,
And he sings to the stars of the jungle nights
   Ere cities were, or laws.

Beast from a world primeval,
   He and his leaping clan,
When the blotched red moon leers over the roofs
   Give voice to their scorn of man.

He will lie on a rug tomorrow
   And lick his silky fur,
And veil the brute in his yellow eyes
   And play he's tame and purr.

But at midnight in the alley
   He will crouch again and wail,
And beat the time for his demon's song
   With the swing of his demon's tail.
                 Don Marquis
                 (1878-1937)

Esther's Tomcat

Daylong this tomcat lies stretched flat
As an old rough mat, no mouth and no eyes,
Continual wars and wives are what
Have tattered his ears and battered his head.

Like a bundle of old rope and iron
Sleeps till blue dusk. Then reappear
His eyes, green as ringstones: he yawns wide red,
Fangs fine as a lady's needle and bright.

A tomcat sprang at a mounted knight,
Locked round his neck like a trap of hooks
While the knight rode fighting its clawing and bite.
After hundred of years the stain's there.

On the stone where he fell, dead of the tom:
That was at Barnborough. The tomcat still
Grallochs odd dogs on the quiet,
Will take the head clean off your simple pullet.

Is unkillable. From the dog's fury,
From gunshot fired point-blank he brings
His skin whole, and whole
From owlish moons of bekittenings

Among ashcans. He leaps and lightly
Walks upon sleep, his mind on the moon.
Nightly over the round world of men,
Over the roofs go his eyes and outcry.

Ted Hughes
(1930-   )

Why so scrawny, cat?
Starving for fat fish or mice . . .
Or backyard love?
Bashō
(1644-1694)

Amorous cat, alas
You too must yowl with your love . . .
Or even worse, without!
Yaha
(1662-1740)

Oh sorry tom-cat
Bigger blacker knights of love
Have knocked you out!
   Shikō
   (1664-1731)

Rash tom-cat lover ...
Careless even of that rice
Stuck to your whiskers
Taigi
(d. 1771)

Arise from sleep, old cat,
And with great yawns and stretchings
Amble out for love.
Issa
(1763-1827)

The
Lover

Cats

A cat is not a person, you say,
not a Christian —
I have seen many!
Playing with mice who sat on their tails
    squeaking out protest
Then let them go
to die by themselves of shock
without wounds other than small claw-marks
little love-bites.

Gunnar Ekelöf
(1907-1968)
translated from the Swedish
by Muriel Rukeyser and
Leif Sjöberg

Woman and Cat

She was playing with her cat
And it was wonderful to see
The white hand and the paw of white
Playing in the dusk at eve.

Now she's hiding, the culprit,
Under tipless black net gloves,
Her murderous claws of agate
Cutting clean as a knife.

And as the other acts, so she, honeyed,
Retracts her deadly claws.
But the devil fears no need

And in the chamber where, sonorous
Rings out her airy laugh
Gleam four points of phosphorus.

Paul Verlaine
(1844-1896)
translated from the French
by G. Michael Bagley

Epitaph on the Duchess of Maine's Cat

Puss passer-by, within this simple tomb
Lies one whose life fell Atropos hath shred;
The happiest cat on earth hath heard her doom,
And sleeps for ever in a marble bed.
Alas! what long delicious days I've seen!
O cats of Egypt, my illustrious sires,
You who on altars, bound with garlands green,
Have melted hearts, and kindled fond desires,
Hymns in your praise were paid, and offerings too,
But I'm not jealous of those rights divine,
Since Ludovisa loved me, close and true,
Your ancient glory was less proud than mine.
To live a simple pussy by her side
Was nobler far than to be deified.

> *La Mothe le Vayer*
> *(1588-1672)*
> *translated from the French*
> *by Edmund Gosse*

The Lover, whose Mistress Feared a Mouse,
Declareth That He Would Become a Cat if
He Might Have His Desire

If I might alter kind,
    What, think you, I would be?
Not Fish, nor Foule, nor Fle, nor Frog,
    Nor Squirrel on the Tree;
The Fish, the Hooke, the Foule
    The lymèd Twig doth catch,
The Fle, the Finger, and the Frog
The Bustard doth dispatch.

The Squirrel thinking nought,
    That feately cracks the nut;
The greedie Goshawke wanting prey,
    In dread of Death doth put;
But scorning all these kindes,
    I would become a Cat,
To combat with the creeping Mouse,
    And scratch the screeking Rat.

I would be present, aye,
    And at my Ladie's call,
To gard her from the fearful Mouse,
    In Parlour and in Hall;
In Kitchen, for his Lyfe,
    He should not shew his hed;
The Pease in Poke should lie untoucht
    When shee were gone to Bed.

The Mouse should stand in Feare,
    So should the squeaking Rat;
All this would I doe if I were
    Converted to a Cat.

                George Turberville
                (1540?-1610)

Nature Notes: Cats

Incorrigible, uncommitted,
They leavened the long flat hours of my childhood,
Subtle, the opposite of dogs,
And, unlike dogs, capable
Of flirting, falling, and yawning anywhere,
Like women who want no contract
But going their own way
Make the way of their lovers lighter.

Louis MacNeice
(1907-1963)

Entry in a Cat's Journal

The love I sent was flying fish —
Returned today —
Stamped and airmailed,
S-w-i-s-h.

> *William E. Harrold*
> *(1936-   )*

The
Friend

Surrender

Let Others praise the cat
And rhapsodize
About her velvet tread
And amber eyes.
I never liked the feline.
Yet, this first cool Fall day,
Before the furnace started,
I looked out upon my door-stoop
And espied a lone gray cat.
Her sinuous back was curled
Around a straying sunbeam
Which seemed to catch and hold her
In a deep and friendly dream.
The sight brought warm comfort
To my lonely flat . . .
Which is a bit more cheerful . . .
Now, that I have a cat.

Evelyn Hickman

To a Cat

I

Stately, kindly, lordly friend,
   Condescend
Here to sit by me, and turn
Glorious eyes that smile and burn,
Golden eyes, love's lustrous meed,
On the golden page I read.

All your wondrous wealth of hair,
   Dark and fair,
Silken-shaggy, soft and bright
As the clouds and beams of night,
Pays my reverent hand's caress
Back with friendlier gentleness.

Dogs may fawn on all and some
   As they come;
You, a friend of loftier mind,
Answer friends alone in kind.
Just your foot upon my hand
Softly bids it understand.

Morning round this silent sweet
   Garden-seat
Sheds its wealth of gathering light,
Thrills the gradual clouds with might,
Changes woodland, orchard, heath,
Lawn, and garden there beneath.

Fair and dim they gleamed below:
   Now they glow
Deep as even your sunbright eyes,
Fair as even the wakening skies.
Can it not or can it be
Now that you give thanks to see?

May not you rejoice as I,
   Seeing the sky
Change to heaven revealed, and bid
Earth reveal the heaven it hid
All night long from stars and moon,
Now the sun sets all in tune?

What within you wakes with day
   Who can say?
All too little may we tell,
Friends who like each other well,
What might haply, if we might,
Bid us read our lives aright.

II

Wild on woodland ways your sires
   Flashed like fires;
Fair as flame and fierce and fleet
As with wings on wingless feet
Shone and sprang your mother, free,
Bright and brave as wind or sea.

Free and proud and glad as they,
   Here today
Rests or roams their radiant child,
Vanquished not, but reconciled,
Free from curb of aught above
Save the lovely curb of love.

Love through dreams of souls divine
   Fain would shine
Round a dawn whose light and song
Then should right our mutual wrong —
Speak, and seal the love-lit law
Sweet Assisi's seer foresaw.

Dreams were theirs; yet haply may
   Dawn a day
When such friends and fellows born,
Seeing our earth as fair at morn,
May for wiser love's sake see
More of heaven's deep heart than we.

Algernon Charles Swinburne
(1837-1909)

The Cats Have Come To Tea

What did she see—oh, what did she see,
As she stood leaning against the tree?
Why, all the cats had come to tea.

What a fine turn-out from round about!
All the houses had let them out,
And here they were with scamper and shout.

"Mew, mew, mew!" was all they could say,
And, "We hope we find you well today."

Oh, what would she do—oh what should she do?
What a lot of milk they would get through;
For here they were with, "Mew, mew, mew!"

She did not know—oh, she did not know,
If bread and butter they'd like or no;
They might want little mice, oh! oh! oh!

Dear me—oh, dear me,
All the cats had come to tea.

Kate Greenaway

The Scholar and His Cat

Each of us pursues his trade,
I and Pangur, my comrade;
His whole fancy on the hunt
And mine for learning ardent.

More than fame I love to be
Among my books, and study;
Pangur does not grudge me it,
Content with his own merit.

When — a heavenly time! — we are
In our small room together,
Each of us has his own sport
And asks no greater comfort.

While he sets his round sharp eye
On the wall of my study,
I turn mine — though lost its edge —
On the great wall of knowledge.

Now a mouse sticks in his net
After some mighty onset,
Then into my store I cram
Some difficult, darksome problem.

When a mouse comes to the kill
Pangur exults — a marvel!
I have, when some secret's won,
My hour of exultation.

Though we work for days or years
Neither the other hinders;
Each is competent and hence
Enjoys his skill in silence.

Master of the death of mice,
He keeps in daily practice;
I, too, making dark things clear,
Am of my trade a master.

Anonymous
(c. 750)
translated from the Irish
by Frank O'Connor

Singular Injustice

I find it most peculiar that
They mock the spinster with her cat,
But beam through sentimental fog
Each time the bachelor walks his dog.
Janet Lloyd

Epitaph

The Death of a Cat

I

Since then, those months ago, these rooms miss something,
A link, a spark, and the street down there reproves
My negligence, particularly the gap
For the new block which, though the pile of timber
Is cleared on which he was laid to die, remains
A gap, a catch in the throat, a missing number.

You were away when I lost him, he had been absent
Six nights, two dead, which I had not learnt until
You returned and asked and found how he had come back
To a closed door having scoured the void of Athens
For who knows what and at length, more than unwell
Came back and less than himself, his life in tatters.

Since when I dislike that gap in the street and that obdurate
Dumb door of iron and glass and I resent
This bland blank room like a doctor's consulting room
With its too many exits, all of glass and frosted,
Through which he lurked and fizzed, a warm retort,
Found room for his bag of capers, his bubbling flasket.

For he was our puck, our miniature lar, he fluttered
Our dovecot of visiting cards, he flicked them askew,
The joker among them who made a full house. As you said,
He was a fine cat. Though how strange to have, as you said later,
Such a personal sense of loss. And looking aside
You said, but unconvincingly: What does it matter?

II

To begin with he was a beautiful object:
Blue crisp fur with a white collar,
Paws of white velvet, springs of steel,
A Pharaoh's profile, a Krishna's grace,
Tail like a questionmark at a masthead
And eyes dug out of a mine, not the dark
Clouded tarns of a dog's, but cat's eyes —
Light in a rock crystal, light distilled
Before his time and ours, before cats were tame.

To continue, he was alive and young,
A dancer, incurably male, a clown,
With his gags, his mudras, his entrechats,
His triple bends and his doubletakes,
Firm as a Rameses in African wonderstone,
Fluid as Krishna chasing the milkmaids,
Who hid under carpets and nibbled at olives,
Attacker of ankles, nonesuch of nonsense,
Indolent, impudent, cat catalytic.

To continue further: if not a person
More than a cipher, if not affectionate
More than indifferent, if not volitive
More than automaton, if not self-conscious
More than mere conscious, if not useful
More than a parasite, if allegorical
More than heraldic, if man-conditioned
More than a gadget, if perhaps a symbol
More than a symbol, if somewhat a proxy
More than a stand-in — was what he was!
A self-contained life, was what he must be
And is not now: more than an object.

And is not now. Spreadeagled on coverlets —
Those are the coverlets, bouncing on chairbacks —
These are the chairs, pirouetting and sidestepping,
Feinting and jabbing, breaking a picture frame —
Here is the picture, tartar and sybarite,
One minute quicksilver, next minute butterballs,
Precise as a fencer, lax as an odalisque,
And in his eyes the light from the mines
One minute flickering, steady the next,
Lulled to a glow or blown to a blaze,
But always the light that was locked in the stone
Before his time and ours; at best semi-precious
All stones of that kind yet, if not precious,
Are more than stones, beautiful objects
But more than objects. While there is light in them.

III

Canyons of angry sound, catastrophe, cataclysm,
Smells and sounds in cataracts, cat-Athens,
Not, not the Athens we know, each whisker buzzing
Like a whole radar station, typhoons of grapeshot,
Crossfire from every roof of ultra-violet arrows
And in every gutter landmines, infra-red,
A massed barrage of too many things unknown
On too many too quick senses (cosseted senses
Of one as spoilt as Pangur Ban, Old Foss
Or My Cat Jeoffry), all the drab and daily
Things to him deadly, all the blunt things sharp,
The paving stones a sword dance. Chanting hawkers
Whose street cries consecrate their loaves and fishes
And huge black chessmen carved out of old priests
And steatopygous boys, they all were Gogs and Magogs
With seven-league battering boots and hair-on-ending voices
Through which he had to dodge. And all the wheels
Of all the jeeps, trucks, trams, motor-bicycles, buses, sports cars,
Caught in his brain and ravelled out his being
To one high horrible twang of breaking catgut,
A swastika of lightning. Such was Athens
To this one indoors cat, searching for what
He could not grasp through what he could not bear,
Dragged to and fro by unseen breakers, broken
At last by something sudden; then dragged back
By his own obstinate instinct, a long dark thread
Like Ariadne's ball of wool in the labyrinth
Not now what he had played with as a kitten
But spun from his own catsoul, which he followed
Now that the minotaur of machines and men
Had gored him, followed it slowly, slowly, until
It snapped a few yards short of a closed door,
Of home, and he lay on his side like a fish on the pavement
While the ball of wool rolled back and down the hill,
His purpose gone, only his pain remaining
Which, even if purpose is too human a word,
Was not too human a pain for a dying cat.

IV

Out of proportion? Why, almost certainly.
You and I, darling, knew no better
Than to feel worse for it. As one feels worse
When a tree is cut down, an ear-ring lost,
A week-end ended, a child at nurse
Weaned. Which are also out of proportion.

Sentimentality? Yes, it is possible;
You and I, darling, are not above knowing
The tears of the semi-, les precious things,
A pathetic fallacy perhaps, as the man
Who gave his marble victory wings
Was the dupe — who knows — of sentimentality,

Not really classic. The Greek Anthology
Laments its pets (like you and me, darling),
Even its grasshoppers; dead dogs bark
On the roads of Hades where poets hung
Their tiny lanterns to ease the dark.
Those poets were late though. Not really classical.

Yet more than an object? Why, most certainly.
You and I, darling, know that sonatas
Are more than sound and that green grass
Is more than grass or green, which is why
Each of our moments as they pass
Is of some moment; more than an object.

So this is an epitaph, not for a calamitous
Loss but for loss; this was a person
In a small way who had touched our lives
With a whisk of delight, like a snatch of a tune
From which one whole day's mood derives.
For you and me, darling, this is an epitaph.

Louis MacNeice
(1907-1963)

Last Words to a Dumb Friend

Pet was never mourned as you,
Purrer of the spotless hue,
Plumy tail, and wistful gaze
While you humoured our queer ways,
Or outshrilled your morning call
Up the stairs and through the hall —
Foot suspended in its fall —
While, expectant, you would stand
Arched, to meet the stroking hand;
Till your way you chose to wend
Yonder, to your tragic end.

Never another pet for me!
Let your place all vacant be;
Better blankness day by day
Than companion torn away.
Better bid his memory fade,
Better blot each mark he made,
Selfishly escape distress
By contrived forgetfulness,
Than preserve his prints to make
Every morn and eve an ache.

From the chair whereon he sat
Sweep his fur, nor wince thereat;
Rake his little pathways out
Mid the bushes roundabout;
Smooth away his talons' mark
From the claw-worn pine-tree bark,
Where he climbed as dusk embrowned,
Waiting us who loitered round.

Strange it is this speechless thing,
Subject to our mastering,
Subject for his life and food
To our gift, and time, and mood;
Timid pensioner of us Powers,
His existence ruled by ours,
Should — by crossing at a breath
Into safe and shielded death,
By the merely taking hence
Of his insignificance —
Loom as largened to the sense,
Shape as part, above man's will,
Of the Imperturbable.

As a prisoner, flight debarred,
Exercising in a yard,
Still retain I, troubled, shaken,
Mean estate, by him forsaken;
And this home, which scarcely took
Impress from his little look,
By his faring to the Dim
Grows all eloquent of him.

Housemate, I can think you still
Bounding to the window-sill,
Over which I vaguely see
Your small mound beneath the tree,
Showing in the autumn shade
That you moulder where you played.

Thomas Hardy
(1840-1928)

Epitaph on a Pet Cat

My life seems dull and flat,
And, as you'll wonder what,
Magny, has made this so,
I want you first to know
It's not for rings or purse
But something so much worse:
Three days ago I lost
All that I value most,
My treasure, my delight;
I cannot speak, or write,
Or even think of what
Belaud, my small grey cat,
Meant to me, tiny creature,
Masterpiece of nature
In the whole world of cats —
And certain death to rats! —
Whose beauty was worthy
Of immortality.

Belaud, first let me say,
Was not entirely grey
Like cats bred at home,
But more like those in Rome,
His fur being silver-grey
And fine and smooth as satin,
While, lying back, he'd display
A white expanse of ermine.
Small muzzle, tiny teeth;
Eyes of a tempered warmth,
Whose pupils of dark-green
Showed every colour seen
In the bow which splendidly
Arches the rainy sky.

Plump neck, short ears, height
To his head proportionate;
Beneath his ebony nostrils
His little leonine muzzle's
Prim beauty, which appeared
Fringed by the silvery beard
Which gave such waggish grace
To his young dandy's face.

His slender leg, small foot —
No lambswool scarf could be
More soft, except when he
Unsheathed and scratched with it!
His neat and downy throat,
Long monkey's tail, and coat
Diversely flecked and freckled,
In natural motley speckled;
His flank and round stomach
Under control, his back
Longish — a Syrian
If ever there was one!

This was Belaud, a gentle
Animal, whose title
To beauty was so sure
He'd no competitor!
A sad and bitter cross!
Irreparable loss!
It almost seems to me
That Death, though he must be
More ruthless than a bear,
Would, if he'd known my rare
Belaud, have felt his heart
Soften — and for my part
I would not wince and shrink
So from life's joys, I think.

But Death has never watched
Him as he jumped or scratched,
Laughed at his nimble tricks,
His many wild frolics,
Admired the sprightly grace
With which he'd turn, or race,
Or, with one whirl of cat,
Tumble, or seize a rat
And play with it — and then
Would make me laugh again
By rubbing at his jaw
With such a frisky paw
In such a dashing manner!
Or when the little monster
Leapt quietly on my bed,
Or when he took his bread

Or meat most daintily
Straight from my lips — for he
Showed in such various ways
His quaint, engaging traits!

What fun to watch him dance,
Scamper, and skate, and prance
After a ball of thread;
To see his silly head
Whirl like a spinning wheel
After his velvet tail;
Or, when he made of it
A girdle, and would sit
Solemnly on the ground,
Showing his fluffy round
Of paunch, seeming to be
Learned in theology,
The spit of some well-known
Doctor at the Sorbonne!
And how, when he was teased,
He used to fence with us —
Yet if we stopped to fuss
Was very soon appeased!

O Magny, now you see
How he diverted me,
You'll realize why I mourn —
And surely no cat born
Has ever had so nice
A style with rats and mice!
He would come unawares
Upon them in their lairs,
And not one could escape
Unless he'd thought to scrape
A second hole — no rat
Ever outran that cat!
And let me add at once
My Belaud was no dunce,
But very teachable,
Knowing how to eat at table —
When offered food, that is:
That eager paw you'd see,
Held out so flirtingly,
Might scratch you otherwise!

Belaud was well-behaved
And in no way depraved;
His only ravages
Were on an ancient cheese,
A finch, and a young linnet
Whose trillings seemed to get
On Belaud's nerves — but then
How perfect are we men?

He wasn't the sort to be
Out everlastingly
After more food to eat,
But was content to wait
Until his meals, when he
Ate without gluttony.

Also he was by nature
A well-conducted creature;
For he would never spread
His traces far and wide
Like many cats, but tried
To live as a well-bred
Feline should live and he
In all his ways cleanly ...

He was my favourite plaything;
And not for ever purring
A long and tunelessly
Grumbling litany,
But kept in his complainings
To kitten-like miaowings.

My only memory
Of him annoying me
Is that, sometimes at night
When rats began to gnaw
And rustle in my straw
Mattress, he'd waken me
Seizing most dexterously
Upon them in their flight.

Now that the cruel right hand
Of Death comes to demand
My bodyguard from me,
My sweet security
Gives way to hideous fears;

Rats come and gnaw my ears,
And mice and rats at night
Chew up the lines I write!

The gods have sympathy
For poor humanity;
An animal's death foretells
Some evil that befalls,
For heaven can speak by these
And other presages.
The day fate cruelly
Took my small dog from me —
My Peloton — the sense
Of evil influence
Filled me with utter dread;
And then I lost my cat:
What crueller storm than that
Could break upon my head!

He was my very dear
Companion everywhere,
My room, my bed, my table,
Even more companionable
Than a little dog; for he
Was never one of those
Monsters that hideously
Fill night with their miaows:
And now he can't become,
Poor little puss, a tom —
Sad loss, by which his splendid
Line is abruptly ended.

God grant to me, Belaud,
Command of speech to show
Your gentle nature forth
In words of fitting worth,
Your qualities to state
In verse as delicate,
That you may live while cats
Wage mortal war on rats.

Joachim du Bellay
(1525-1560)
translated from the French
by R. N. Currey

Ode on the Death of a Favourite Cat, Drowned in a Tub of Gold Fishes

'Twas on a lofty vase's side,
Where China's gayest art had dyed
   The azure flowers, that blow;
Demurest of the tabby kind,
The pensive Selima reclined,
   Gazed on the lake below.

Her conscious tail her joy declared;
The fair round face, the snowy beard,
   The velvet of her paws,
Her coat, that with the tortoise vies,
Her ears of jet, and emerald eyes,
   She saw; and purr'd applause.

Still had she gazed; but 'midst the tide
Two angel forms were seen to glide,
   The Genii of the stream:
Their scaly armour's Tyrian hue
Through richest purple to the view
   Betray'd a golden gleam.

The hapless Nymph with wonder saw:
A whisker first and then a claw,
   With many an ardent wish,
She stretch'd in vain to reach the prize.
What female heart can gold despise?
   What Cat's averse to fish?

Presumptuous Maid! with looks intent
Again she stretch'd, again she bent,
   Nor knew the gulf between.
(Malignant Fate sat by, and smiled)
The slippery verge her feet beguiled,
   She tumbled headlong in.

Eight times emerging from the flood
She mew'd to every watery God,
   Some speedy aid to send.
No Dolphin came, no Nereid stirred:
Nor cruel *Tom*, nor *Susan* heard.
   A fav'rite has no friend!

From hence, ye Beauties, undeceived,
Know, one false step is ne'er retrieved,
   And be with caution bold.
Not all that tempts your wandering eyes
And heedless hearts, is lawful prize;
   Nor all that glisters, gold.
                 Thomas Gray
                 (1716-1771)

On the Death of a Cat
A Friend of Mine Aged Ten Years and a Half

Who shall tell the lady's grief
When her Cat was past relief?
Who shall number the hot tears
Shed o'er her, belov'd for years?
Who shall say the dark dismay
Which her dying caused that day?

Come, ye Muses, one and all,
Come obedient to my call;
Come and mourn with tuneful breath
Each one for a separate death;
And, while you in numbers sigh,
I will sing her elegy.

Of a noble race she came,
And Grimalkin was her name.
Young and old full many a mouse
Felt the prowess of her house;
Weak and strong full many a rat
Cowered beneath her crushing pat;
And the birds around the place
Shrank from her too-close embrace.
But one night, reft of her strength,
She lay down and died at length:
Lay a kitten by her side
In whose life the mother died.
Spare her life and lineage,
Guard her kitten's tender age,
And that kitten's name as wide
Shall be known as hers that died.
And whoever passes by
The poor grave where Puss doth lie,
Softly, softly let him tread,
Nor disturb her narrow bed.

Christina Rossetti
(1830-1894)

Atossa
An extract from "Poor Matthias"

Poor Matthias! Wouldst thou have
More than pity? claim'st a stave?
— Friends more near us than a bird
We dismiss'd without a word.
Rover, with the good brown head,
Great Atossa, they are dead;
Dead, and neither prose nor rhyme
Tells the praises of their prime.
Thou didst know them old and grey,
Know them in their sad decay.
Thou hast seen Atossa sage
Sit for hours beside thy cage;
Thou wouldst chirp, thou foolish bird,
    Rover died — Atossa too.
Less than they to us are you!
Flutter, chirp — she never stirr'd!
What were now these toys to her?
Down she sank amid her fur;
Eyed thee with a soul resign'd —
And thou deemedst cats were kind!
— Cruel, but composed and bland,
Dumb, inscrutable and grand,
So Tiberius might have sat,
Had Tiberius been a cat.

Nearer human were their powers,
Closer knit their life with ours.
Hands had stroked them, which are cold,
Now for years, in churchyard mould;
Comrades of our past were they,
Of that unreturning day.
Changed and aging, they and we
Dwelt, it seem'd, in sympathy.
Alway from their presence broke
Somewhat which remembrance woke
Of the loved, the lost, the young —
Yet they died, and died unsung.
                    Matthew Arnold
                    (1822-1888)

An Elegy to Oscar, a Dead Cat

Damn'd be this harsh mechanick age
    That whirls us fast and faster,
And swallows with Sabazian rage
    Nine lives in one disaster.

I take my quill with sadden'd thought,
    Tho' falt'ringly I do it;
And, having curst the Juggernaut,
    Inscribe: OSCARVS FVIT!
                H. P. Lovecraft
                (1890-1937)

ACKNOWLEDGMENTS

"A Cat" from *A Far Land* by Martha Ostenso, copyright 1924 by Thomas Seltzer, Inc., reprinted by permission of Roy C. Durkin.

"A Cat" from *Collected Poems* by Edward Thomas, copyright Faber & Faber Ltd., and Myfanwy Thomas.

"The Cat" from *Façade* by Dame Edith Sitwell, reprinted by permission of Gerald Duckworth & Co. Ltd., and David Higham Associates, Ltd.

"The Cat and the Moon" from *The Collected Poems of W. B. Yeats*, copyright 1919 by Macmillan Publishing Company, Inc. Reprinted by permission of Mr. M. B. Yeats, the Macmillan Company of Canada Ltd., the Macmillan Publishing Company of New York, and A. P. Watt & Son.

·"Cats" from *Selected Poems of Gunnar Ekelöf*, copyright by Twayne Publishers, Inc.

"Cats" from *Selection* by A. S. J. Tessimond. Reprinted by permission of the Estate of A. S. J. Tessimond.

"Cats and Kings" from *Collected Poems* by Alfred Noyes, copyright 1906, renewed 1934 by Alfred Noyes. Reprinted by permission of Harper & Row, Publishers, Inc., and John Murray (Publishers) Ltd.

"cheerio, my deario" from *archy and mehitabel* by Don Marquis, copyright 1927 by Doubleday & Company, Inc. Reprinted by permission of Doubleday & Company, Inc. and Faber and Faber Ltd.

"The Death of a Cat" by Louis MacNeice. Reprinted by permission of Faber & Faber Ltd. from *The Collected Poems of Louis MacNeice*.

"A Dirge for a Righteous Kitten" from *The Collected Poems of Vachel Lindsay*, copyright 1914 by Macmillan Publishing Company, Inc.

"An Elegy to Oscar, A Dead Cat" reprinted from *Selected Letters*, Vol. II, by H. P. Lovecraft, copyright 1968. Reprinted by permission of the Estate of August Derleth.

"Entry in a Cat's Journal" by William E. Harrold. Originally appeared in *Green Apple: A Review of the Arts*, Fall, 1969; reprinted by permission of William E. Harrold.

"Esther's Tomcat" from *Lupercal* by Ted Hughes, copyright © 1960 by Ted Hughes. Originally appeared in *The New Yorker;* reprinted by permission of Harper & Row Publishers, Inc., and Faber & Faber Ltd.